BROKEN HALVES OF A MILKY SUN

BROKEN HALVES
OF A MILKY SUN

POEMS

AAIÚN NIN

ASTRA HOUSE | NEW YORK

Astra House
A Division of Astra Publishing House
astrahouse.com
Printed in the United States of America

Publisher's Cataloging-in-Publication data
Names: Nin, Aaiún, author.
Title: Broken halves of a milky sun : poems. / Aaiún Nin
Description: New York, NY: Astra House, 2022.
Identifiers: LCCN: 2021917257 | ISBN: 9781662600791 (hardcover) |
9781662600807 (ebook)
Subjects: LCSH Angolan poetry. | Gender nonconformity—Poetry—
21st century. | Africa—Emigration and immigration—Poetry. |
Poetry—21st century. | BISAC POETRY / African | POETRY / LGBTQ+
Classification: LCC PR9408.A53 .N56 2022 | DDC 811.6—dc23

First edition
10 9 8 7 6 5 4 3 2 1

Design by Richard Oriolo
The text is set in Filosofia.
The titles are set in Gotham.

This is for the Black girls.

This is for the Liability Crew honeys:
Yance Maya, Mihaela Yordanova,
Sasha West, Janna Aldaraji, Andrea Coloma,
and my two sister-wives Irlin Osaland and
Patricia Bbaale-Bandak. I could have not
done this without you. Thank you for
teaching me how transformative love is.
You are truly my heart.

CONTENTS

BROKEN HALVES OF A MILKY SUN

Black skin in the forsaken outback
of the world
both concrete and jungle
in varying states of decomposition
and men in a corner
ordering girls to smile
stiff with rigor mortis
all bones no flesh

girls in prim clothes
going to school
going to church
going to graveyards
in prim clothes.
Stone eyed
missing teeth
blueblack skin
huddled together
bathed in molestation.

The first dying.

In a mass grave
a blueblack shadow is born.
In a room smelling of kerosene lamps.
To women in their fourth dying
and men sitting outside drinking beer.
Holographic.

Horror makes the body transparent.
Forbidden flesh
perpetuating unbecoming
algor mortis
the long fallen
broken screens.
Holographic.

Going to school
where a white god is nailed to a cross
promising paradise
abandoning the living
knowing it's the dead who teach us how to count.

Heavy hands of grown people.
Covering their mouths.
Scream in silence.

The first dying.
Body is a body
Body is a body
Flesh is not yours
Growing flesh of adolescence.
Unripe flesh ready for picking.

So we grow
holding hands with the reaper.
Dispossessed from body and land.
In makeshift homes

deleting the human part of ourselves.

Screening

ctrl+alt+del

esc

del

Funneled through algorithms

where numbers and letters are the same

where numbers cancel out names

and news of dead Black people

makes us spin with no god to welcome them into paradise.

Unbaptized corpses. Unholy flesh.

Heartbreak is stone-faced

mechanical

fingers on the trigger of whatever shape a gun will take

shoots in the dark

ctr+del

self-destructs

esc+del

fighting against the will to live.

Unfolding.

Subjugate the law of false nature

reimagining happiness

a Black happiness

filled with sorrow

too many fucked-up memories

of us as children

going to school
going to church
going to graveyards
in prim clothes.
Funeral wear.
Whipping joy into existence

the bones of the hopeful dead
rattling in their caskets
cheering on from beyond the abyss

bodies in a circle
hollering.
Sometimes smiling.
Smiling still.
Maybe out of hope
ardent wakefulness

that some of us
can stick to the first dying
push against the second third fourth
hold on to whatever flesh is left
call it our own
heartbroken
still smiling
maybe out of delirium.

A door left ajar
movement between the stillness
the movement
as a slit
confined within two walls
momentarily
which is to say
choice
doors opened wide
or sealed shut
when spaces hold secrets
secrets held. menace
formed by bodies
silence. menace
silence is silence
a prison. menace
incision on a wall
slit
what strength we must have to hold secrets
inside the body
nerve endings. muscle. fat. cartilage. skin. tongue. vulva.
slit.
postural changes
impact
trauma weighs on the body
language
as communication
for communicating. lingua.

as in tongue. as in mother tongue.

lingua as muscle. as tongue. as language.

lingua. as vessel. as tool for conveying information.

trauma. release

lingua as contraction of muscle.

between slits.

hosted inside the mouth.

lingua as organ.

lingua as tongue

placed between legs.

lingua as rope.

lingua on clit.

clit pulsating on

lingua

nerve endings. muscle. skin. vulva. cum.

language as release.

space

between walls.

contraction. contra action. against the grain.

what release must the body crave

absence. no sense.

sensation contrary to custom. pulsating. slits crevices tight spaces.

language as release. release as. release.

lingua as tongue. in tight spaces.

muscular contractions. between slits.

enter thought. memory. anima.

what animates the body

beating heart.

stitched arteries.

a complex central nervous system.
bacterial ecosystems.
the skin that houses it all
blackblue purple bruises
what animates the body
split communication
immediate communication
brain cells
immediate signals
pulsations
on blueblack purple skin
information as memory
stored on the body
language as a motor skill
speech as contraction of muscle
release must not be silent
bodies are not concrete.

God gave man the word
And in the word was his name
Man took the word and interpreted it
In his likeness
The likeness only of the man

The word condemned the woman
And the soil where the body of the murdered lesbian lay
Soaked her blood
Absolved her from the justice she would not receive
In the name of God was she killed
And in the name of God will her murderer be forgiven
In the land of the free
Where we are equals before the law

Yet it is more righteous to kill the innocent
To blame the victim and forgive the rapist
In the name of God
Laws are made to justify the killing of entire races of people
And in the name of God
European governments are absolved of their inaction
When the dead bodies wash up on the shores of their continent

There is no limit to the condemnation of this word
And the loathing that seeps
Into the core of those subjugated by it
The word of God taught women to hate themselves
And seek supremacy in the oppression of others
To look for redemption in violence
Condone violence committed against other women

In the name of God

They threw acid on the brown face of a man suspected of being gay
And strangled the transwoman on the passenger seat of an old car

Always in the name
And the unlikeness that justifies the violence
Eternal damnation awaits the woman
The negro
The homo
With no place to stand in the land of the free
Where it is more righteous to kill the innocent
To blame the victim and forgive the rapist

In the name of God

Pray for us now and in the hour of our death
Pray for us now and in the hour of our death
Pray for us now and in the hour of our death
Pray for us.

Luanda smells of heat
dust
Fumes from exhaust pipes
and sweat
It smells of fried dough
and putrefied waters that host mosquito larvae
It smells of the sea
and spillages from oil rigs
Of cheaply tarred roads
and, faintly, of urine.

Luanda has the sounds of
Semba, Kizomba and KuDuro
Of bus fare collectors
screaming their routes across the city.
Katandeiras calling out the catch of the day
and the voices of drowsy security guards
complaining about the oppressive heat.

Luanda looks like
blossoming acacia trees
and derelict colonial buildings
collapsing with time and brick rot.

Skyscrapers and
blue-and-white combis
that transport people packed like tinned fish
children in white robes going to school
police officers pimping themselves out for bribes
and banks with too-long queues.

Gleaming black skin walking at a fast pace
counterfeit iPhones and
Cuca.

She sits on the red dust
beneath acacia trees.
It has not rained for months.
Golden leaves fall around her.
She smiles when approached,
dusting her fruits.
She sits there every day,
her fruit rotting before it is sold.

The soil is the color of ochre.
Abandoned construction sites ghost
over the city.
Sentinels of forgotten hope.
There are trees with dried-up leaves
and empty plastic bags caught in branches.
Smoke rises into the early evening,
from piles of burning filth.
Women set up stalls,
Their faces illuminated
by fire lamps made from beer bottles.

1.

You learn from women
early on
to not play cards at the devil's table
To not look straight into the eyes of men
lest they take you

Keep your legs closed
be good with your hands and learn quickly
Cry
when no one can see you
eat the pain and
never think this life is yours to live

On Sundays I went to mass with belt marks on my legs
White Jesus on the cross who died to save us from our skin
Transfiguration of self-loathing
The blood shed on this altar
as a sacrifice to the gods of greed that
lay dormant behind a silver crucifixion
Eat its body
Drink its blood and
pray for skin light enough to be loved

The virgin stares ahead
unmoved by tears
of children too young
to feel worthless

with faces
deepened with time
and eyes
downcast to avoid attention

Women are meant to be gentle
More caring
less violent
As if we have not learnt to eroticize our pain
Blind
suffocated rage
That lies screaming in the abdomen
An inheritance of remembrance etched onto us
Blow after blow

There are some things
women brought up
fearful and devout
must never crave
Whisperings of the body that cling to skin
Slow fevers that entice stirrings
In tight spaces
Women with too many secrets
brought up
devout and fearful
Should not be this way.

2.

We're all serpents in the grass
Too true to stay stuck in time mourning the past
Raging in the present with no space to be restored
A lifetime seeing red makes us bitter
Poisoned by black bile of disingenuous smiles
This world cannot decide my fate

I move
Beyond the dashikis
The intricate names of Yoruba gods
carved statues of nubile women on black wood
The resentment of the displaced
I renounce the silence
and reclaim a voice
Black as fuck

Head too high
blowing kisses
at scowling faces
Running free enough to fall for someone with shady eyes
Heal what's to heal from a life measured by sighs
things end too quickly to live behind the scenes

You learn from women
early on
that we all need kindness
To look for the stories
in women with downcast eyes

the devil is a lie that disappears behind smoke

and life

is a long journey towards forgiveness.

We are the bodies who fled
We are the dead bodies
washed ashore.
Our bloated bodies, if they find them,
are mute and nameless
desperation dissipated,
silenced.
Drowned in saltwater.

The sea.
Crowded boats.
Orange vests.
Drowning Africans.

Those who fled were sent back.
It is now illegal to seek refuge.
The Black and brown quota in Europe has been filled.
The Mediterranean Sea is now a mass grave.

Supplications fall to silent ears
As the perceived inferiority
Tinges the skin of those bodies who fled.
Our bodies,
the bloated bodies.
Remembered, if at all,
As gross, violent
Hardly human.

Orange vests.
The sea.
Drowning people.

Fleeing war is fleeing is fleeing war is fleeing war is fleeing war is fleeing war is fleeing war is fleeing war is fleeing war is fleeing war is fleeing war is fleeing war is fleeing war is fleeing war is fleeing war is fleeing war is fleeing war is fleeing war is fleeing war is fleeing is fleeing war is fleeing

Activist spaces littered with non-Black people of color who have not reckoned with their internalized white supremacy and silence the shit out of Black people are as good as used condoms at a skinhead barbecue.

Mourning is movement.
Mourning is to feel sorrow
For loss.
For the passing of people.
For tragedies and deep misfortunes
It is to feel sadness.
Hopelessness.
Rage.
Insanity.
Rage.
Above all things rage.
It is not to sit still and wait
for justice.
To mourn is to move
It is to name, yes
to name
and not forget.
It is closure.
Acknowledgment.

Grief is not static.
There is no dissonance
between mourning
and organizing.

We mourn
because we are human
to acknowledge that we are human
and that those who have died

At the hands of those who breed injustice
Are human.
And deserve to be treated as humans.
Mourning is to not forget.
As people whose history has been erased
We cannot afford to forget.
And we forget
when the vulnerable are discouraged
From speaking
any words that express pain
And the insurmountable grief
that floods out
That makes us act.
Mourning is an act.
It is not something that happens onto us.
Mourning is an act.

Black people have taken to the streets of the world
Screaming that our lives matter
Enraged.
Because of grief.
In an act of mourning.

Grief is not static.
To mourn is an act of power
Protest.
Here
where we are not considered people.

Who will mourn for us
If we don't do it ourselves?
Who will make us human,
if we don't do it ourselves?

And treated like we do not exist.
We exist.
Yes, we exist
in parenthesis
we exist
In mourning we exist.

My mother's face set inwards
She walks in the tired way my grandmother walks—
swaying from side to side
as if gently pulled by ghosts.

She smiles in the brief manner those plagued
with worry and sorrow do—a quick stretch of her lips
as if ghostly hands pulled at her face.

My mother cries in secret
and shouts at me to deflect
that I was a child when I saw her crying
and children must not see mothers cry.

Have you forgotten? We were in a room
crowded with people
and music so loud we spoke with our bodies.
You breathed on my neck,
pressed your finger inside
my open mouth.
I dug my nails into your skin.
Have you forgotten? Or maybe we were outside
On a stifling summer night
we kissed on a balcony and
I put my hands inside your clothes
and felt you throb
(you tasted of salt. your hands were perfect)
Have you forgotten what I taste like?
My skin was as warm as your breath
you held me pressed up against the wall
and I suffocated your name
in the sounds of rustling leaves.
We were in a room
with music so loud we spoke with our bodies. Do you remember?
Perhaps
this was another room
in another evening

you looked so beautiful
it broke my heart.
I loved you in those moments
when neither of us said anything and

the only thing that mattered was
the urgency in the closeness of our
gleaming bodies.
Dancing with you
liquid
right after
being pressed between you and a damp wall.

The sound of it is "Waweh"

There is a story . . . well . . . there are many stories . . . but there is
one in particular that echoes. In my country, this story, it echoes
everywhere. The sound of it is "Waweh"

. . . and you hear it when a woman has collapsed on the ground
because her child passed away
but the ground has no asphalt
so she collapsed on the dirt
and the dirt picks up as dust in the air
xinguila, mãe. o teu filho morreu.

O teu filho morreu
and her pano has come undone
and everyone can see her bare legs
now covered in dust
and there is no money
and when she looks hard
she finds just enough for dinner
mas agora tem que comprar caixa p'ra criança

and because there is no money
the box is the cheapest she could find
and when she saw her child again
neatly dressed
and eyes closed
she collapsed again
but there was rough cement on the floor

so she bruised herself
the skin on her knees lifted
Waweh, waweh! O meu filho
O meu filho, waweh! Meu filho de sofrimento
waweh!

and when she collapses
and does not move again
her family is around her
and she is picked up and placed on a mattress
that smells of children who wet the bed
with crisp, clean sheets
And she sleeps hoping to not wake up
And when she does
she can hear the neighbor's children playing
Margarida Morena
vende a sua farinha
Margarida Morena
vende a sua farinha

Ilinguilé, ilinguilé, ilinguilé ilinguilé

And after the funeral
she will continue mourning
and after that, those who came to pay respects
will return to their own homes
to the children they did not lose
and this woman

she will keep echoing
Waweh!
At first loudly
but in time
Only her eyes will say it.

ai, ai, ai ainda estou a peneirar
ainda estou a peneirar
com uma linda peneira
Ai!
Ai, ai, ai ainda estou a peneirar
ainda estou a peneirar
com uma linda peneira

Margarida Morena
vende a sua farinh,
Margarida Moren,
vende a sua farinha . . .

A crucified man condemned us all.

Shaking hands
It means hello
Apology
Flesh pressed against flesh
(hold still for long enough and feel it pulsate)
Uncomfortable handshakes
with their thin films of cold sweat disjoining skin from skin
Hands
Arms outstretched aching to be pulled back
Interlocked fingers
The caress of a thumb on opposing skin
Insignificant gestures
carrying the weight of the world
It means hello
Reassurance
Hold a hand firmly and briefly
with a direct gaze
A soft gaze
The squeezed hand relaxes under the firm grip
Insignificant gestures
(carrying the weight of the world).

Tell me of the first time you were poisoned.

When deep red blood turned to crude oil. Black and heavy.

And your soul split in half.

And those halves splintered further, so you exist in fragments.

it was dark inside the plane.

I cried in that way my aunt taught me how to cry,

silently

holding my face to the side so no one can see it

breathing in the smell of airplane food, greasy and metallic

Show me a wound that never healed. Show me bruises

that stain your skin like birthmarks.

Show me those scars, that by some grace

are swollen

and have turned pearlescent

on the blackness of your skin.

in the name of the father

the son

and the holy spirit

the belt strikes.

always on my body. never on my face.

Tell me a secret.

Show me where shame sits on your body.

With your finger trace what it looks like on your skin.

With your fingers show me what it feels like to be wanted.

With you finger trace the outlines of your smile.

where is your home?

Is there a time when you forget the putrid taste of humiliation?

Little sister asked what's wrong with our mother
Little sister asked why is our mother crying
Little sister can't get out of bed
Little sister has pneumonia
We have not seen our father in six months

How do you measure loss?
tell me of the things you hope to forget.
of the things you hoped you would become
before you were taken from yourself.
of the things that made you cruel.
tell me when you realized
that going forward means letting go
of the parts of yourself you once loved.

Mother writes to me saying I should call father.
What she is saying is call me.
What she is saying is go back in time.
What she is saying is you were never mine.
What she is saying is I want to be yours.

How must we keep ourselves together
when the universal patterns of migration
make themselves hosts to our agency to stay still
and we are blown apart by gusts of wind
laden with dust
laden with wails

smelling faintly of gunpowder and famine
forcing us into hostile places
that transform us into number sequences printed in cards
and A4 pieces of paper
barcodes with details
of our unwanted migrant histories
and criminal records
when the crime committed is reaching for safety

I have tried many times to fall asleep
hoping to forget all that I have lived
thinking that none of my jokes are actually funny
they are simply tragedies I have learned to laugh at.
And if I believed in God
I'd wish for three apples to fall from heaven.
One for you.
One for me.
And one for whomever decides our fate.

1.

Language must be adequate.

Years ago,
my sister came to visit me
she wore a yellow dress
and we lay in the grass until our skin
itched.
She said
in a hoarse voice
Will you come back with us
   No
Dad had an accident
everyone thought he was going to die
   Did you cry
A little

Tell me everything you remember since I left
her hair was still damp when we fell asleep
sharing the same pillow.
She wore the same yellow dress when she left.

Yes. Years ago,
it can only be years ago
we were children then
not anymore
she said

I wish you had not left

Sometimes
when I speak to Mother over the phone
I tell her that
I want to go back
she tells me
If you cry on the phone again,
I will not speak with you

2.
Years ago,
A woman told me
I had the devil inside of me
Because a grown man
forced himself on me
and I kept it a secret

once,
twice,
an eternity
and times never mattered
when once should not have happened.
If you tell anyone . . .

I was six years old.

3.

Shame is learned behavior
Silence and fear become culture
Silence then becomes a prison
and I have hated myself for the shame I have felt
   If I could tell someone . . .

Years ago,
   I was asleep and a man came
   there was so much pain
            I could not even scream.

And now
there is no shame
I have learned
silence is a prison
and so is fear

4.

A beautiful man helped me.

He said
this also happened to me
maybe fifteen years ago
and you are the only one
I have ever told

we kissed on the lips when
we said goodbye

I cried so much that night

I got a nosebleed
Today
I cry a lot less than I should

5.
It has not been many years since
a woman pinned me down
desire and then a spasm
my bedsheets felt like broken glass
    wrap your legs around me
she said
her head tilted back
    come closer
if I were laying on broken glass
I wonder if my skin would break
    does skin break when there is no fear
    would surrender keep it from tearing.

6.
Language must be adequate

At first it might not . . .
. . . but then it becomes
it must

if we are to speak about violence
and if we are to speak about longing
if we are to speak about silence

and if we cannot speak then we must write
and if we cannot write
return to speech
before we turn into something altogether different
listen, listen . . .
return to speech
before we turn
   into something altogether different.

We consume the body during sex

spit out

contracted breath

strings of profanities

trails of saliva on skin sweat

        the salty taste of sex

the acrid weight of depression

temporarily lifted

bent. over

in a small cubicle

made-up face pressed

against wall

index ring

finger deep inside

mating animals primordial beasts. entranced by the pulse of a

body on a body, body on all fours

engorged member

ramming (rimming)

weakened knees gush of fluid

drip

white. transparent

drip

release. shout.

bodies collapsed cottonmouth dry lips wet cunt

immobile

      an

      imagined trail

         of smoke

           lingering scent of fucking

consume the body during sex. slow

soft quickening pulse

slow soft tongue

spit wave. split

apart

legs apart

dissect the body with tongue. with finger. with the smooth hard.

   with lips pin the body

lick the markings on the skin

spit words split worlds

contracted muscles pour fluid. cunt fluid floods the body

silken crevices white transparent

tongue tight behind swollen lips pinkish flesh

cum against death's slight breeze

white foam atop waves. nature's force

fracturing the fabric of human constitution

carnal. only carnal

    without mystery, with necessity

staccato release of bodies

arched

bent over

erect pressed against a wall

milky liquid running down

languidity of orgasm soft bruises, deeper breath.

Life will hit you, but you already know that
It will break your heart
There will be times when thoughts of dying will seem more comforting
than waking up to live another day
This pain will transform you
This pain will remind you
You are alive
There is pain so profound that
there is no medicine strong enough to heal from it in one lifetime
And when you fall, find those who care enough to listen
who give you a plate of food
a place to sleep
Hold you when you are in the thralls of torment
because no matter how much you try
your body will always be too small
to hold on to so much pain
without tearing itself apart.

If youth is wasted on the young
Mine has already gone to waste.

I am thinking of killing myself
This is not a fair solution.
Still,
I am thinking of killing myself

I am buried in a bed
ornamented with books,
with clothes, with empty bottles
With a screen and muted voices
I cannot sleep.

I cannot sleep and I cannot run

I am thinking of killing myself
I cannot remove the weighted coat
This shapeless coat
That cements me in silent insanity
That hardens my skin
The inevitable headache
Stomach pains
Sweaty palms and heaviness of limbs
Tear stained eyes
Closed
Nails digging into skin
Skin released before it breaks

I am thinking of killing myself

I have run out of space to further mutilate myself
The air is stale with the scent of putrefying grief
I lay in bedsheets that smell of sweat
And sex I regret having
Intoxicating myself in the circular chaos
Staring deeply into nothing

Often
I think of my mother and sisters
the light of faces gathered over dinner tables
Laughter hanging in the air
Delicate as dandelion seeds blowing in the wind

I am thinking of killing myself

Some days,
when it is easier to breathe,
I have glimpses of how I used to be
How it feels to stand on my own feet
And not be afraid of falling apart
And when asked how I am doing
I can answer that I am doing all right
Without feeling like an absolute failure
And crack the windows open
And air out the room
water the plants
And launder my bedsheets

and the sweatpants I have worn for days
That smell of paint and jerking off
And listen to the rain beating across the windows
Like grains of salt
Giving sound
To the sluggish melancholy
Of wintertime in Copenhagen
And wash away the sordid mask of my insanity.

There are two bodies with no heads
intertwined together
closing their fists around unsoiled promises
yet to be broken
by the cold swiftness of time
hands sweeping through bare torso
necks bent sharply to the side
kissed
in a darkened room
of a derelict city house
with broken floorboards and no heating
depression has made me lose my head
and I have become something simpler
a heartbeat
these bodies do not notice
the blackened mold on ivory white walls
spores exploding all about the room
in a storm of sordid dust
that settles on the skin
and we do not brush away.

Your room is cold and dark
Anxiously neat
It smells faintly of soap and deodorant
It smells of clean laundry
dry soil
in potted plants that need to be watered
And quickly we are naked

Sometimes lust is not so bad.
It was a curious thing to see you undress
Granted we were strangers to each other
Made familiar
By the dizzying conversations we had in a bar
We had both surrendered
To the truth that
Our respective pains
would never put together the pieces of our yesterdays
So there is this
(You asked me what I wanted
I said I wanted to have sex with you)

You are someone I wrote to
We met in a graveyard
Talked briefly
And had sex the entire afternoon
We fell asleep like that
In stretched sheets
Limbs sprawled about

My head resting on your thigh
(It was nothing else.
We just wanted to fuck each other)

We met in a café
Our existences transient
Split between continents
Belonging only to time
And briefly to desire

It is a funny thing, intimacy
That we can spend hours
Days together
And still feel so foreign to each other
As if the fleeting nature
Of our encounter
Lacks the needed substance
To transform sex into something more
The pardoned obscenities of our fingers
Sign a mutual agreement that we will never be parts of each other
There was only lust.

I write to slow the passing of time
watching days and savoring the salt
I write to teach myself not to flinch when tenderness is shown
And surrender to things I might never understand
I write because love is volatile
And hides itself in the strangest of places
I write because I am not made out of pain
And I am more than the battles I have fought.
I write because being Black is fucking awesome
I write because there is power in existing in the alternative
I write because I have taped a knife to the back of my head
And you will never see me bow
I write because silence has not saved me
I write because I'm sick of dying
I write because I'm mad as hell
I write because I'm fly as fuck
I write because I love mad sex
I write because I'm Black as hell
I fucked myself and gave birth to power
I write because I am human
I write because despite suffering from racism,
homophobia,
border regimes,
being beaten,
raped
and incarcerated
I still choose Black
I write because I will always choose Black

I write because I get to be Black
I write because I love being Black
I write because I want Black love
Because I want Black joy
Because I want Black drip
Because I want Black health
I write because I belong in this world
I write because I am exhausted by my rage
I write because I refuse to be broken
I write because I am fly as fuck
Because I'm mad as fuck
Because I'm Black as hell.

Find some real chilies
the kind that release that pungent smell
that makes some people cough when
they are bruised
or cut open.

pull out the stalks
leave them whole if they are small
cut them up if they are big
put them in a jar
with garlic
a whole bay leaf
and salt
top it up with some good agua ardente
and let it sit in a dark place for
at least two weeks

where I am from
this is called
molho de jindungo
it is eaten with all things savory
it is strong and sour
pungent and a little sweet
the sweat it brings
is an exorcism on the insipid palates of colonial foods
this is not something that flatters pale skin
and its bland constitution
accustomed to boiled potatoes
and unseasoned meat

this is flavor that is bold
and without apology
this is flavor that is too strong
to be appropriated by the absence of melanin
this is not to be purchased
in trendy, sterile, organic food stores around Copenhagen
next to quinoa
soy milk
and frozen açaí berries
whose immoderate demand
from white, western bodies
only contributes to
environmental devastation and
the exploitation of indigenous communities

this is found in people's homes
made by a mother
an uncle
a grandmother
a father
and not
a gentrifier

this is medicine for your soul
this is food that brings
folks back
to dreams of ancestral pasts
that pinches them into familiarity
this is the bride

of Calulu, Mufete
and Muamba
this is food that
remains unflinching to
the scorn and disdain
of ignorant people
whose distorted sense of culture
exists as result of theft
And claiming ownership
of what does not belong to them

cooking becomes an act of conjure
when chopped onions and garlic frying on a pan
bring you home
when fried onions and garlic
have become brown enough
that cleaned and roughly shredded pumpkin leaves
are thrown into the pan
and tossed until they wilt
and their color changes into
the deep emerald green
that is often disliked by children
and finished off with raw peanut paste
and the wooden spoon
that stirs this
is tapped on a hand
and this hand with a small drop of sauce
is brought up to an expecting mouth
just a taste

the rich flavor
sends a visceral nod of approval

it is conjure
when food is cooked
with love
it is conjure when food
is an incantation
of histories
that instability
wars
displacement
and diasporic experiences
can make us forget

food that is strong and bold
is a continuation of history
it is resistance
preservation
that brings us forward
a celebration of identity

so when you find yourself
lost and gaslighted by a society
that functions for your peril
and you need to eat something
that will remind you where you are from
find a jar filled
with the kind of

chilies that release a pungent smell
that makes white people cough
when they are bruised or cut open
with the stalks pulled out
whole if they are small
cut up if they are big
with garlic
a whole bay leaf
and salt
topped up with some good agua ardente
and left to sit in a dark place for
at least two weeks.

We are the broken halves of a milky sun
Who do not dream the same dreams
We inhale the same air as crows
Soft as raw cotton
Stiffened in a stitch
To breathe is to convulse
The dystopic future is this moment

A plague of locusts on treasured crops

The ever constant
Sprayed over with insecticides
That grow harsher by the day
And poisons the grass
And poisons the well
And poisons the bodies
Of the We that are covered in mud
We that know gunshots
We that left school
We that fled home
We that crossed the deep blue Atlantic
The We that are Nigeria Benin Ghana
We that live and survive We that die
We that are dying like the forests of the Congo
Missing limbs
Malnutrition
Cobalt mines

Dystopia is 1471
Dystopia is Prince Henry
Dystopia is laying six feet under with bullet wounds

The present is drowning in saltwater
    The present is asylum camps
        The present is war
            The present is separation
                The present is being auctioned in the Sahara

The present is being imprisoned for fleeing war
    The present is fleeing war

The ever constant is a Holy Book

Dystopia is colonialism
Dystopia is narcoterrorism
Dystopia is opium fields
Dystopia is addiction

Dystopia is the present
The present is a failing economy
The present is genocide of indigenous people
A holocaust left in the shadows
The present is terror
The present is human and insect feeding on the same digested hymen

The present is rage
The present is protest
The present is necrotic
The past is homophobic
So is the present

And we inhale the same air as crows.

If we happen to meet on this road
In this dusty, transient place
The space between shelter and rejection
We are far from home

The routines we learned in our previous lives are broken
We must forge new language
New patterns
To describe the uncertainty
That paves our respective paths

The vague nature of the hope
To not lose more than what we had

There is harsh wisdom in our calcified bones
We remember the wailing and screaming
We remember the wind
Far more clearly than peace

The ocean, the forest and the desert
Have turned into mass graves
    So we must leave

The sneer and disdain
Of existing as intruders
Far from home
Pre-cadavers
Casualties of ejaculations
From the wrong types of bodies
Punished for not being dead yet

We learned early that to exist is to feel discomfort
Here
or there
no longer matters
We must be still and keep moving
Doused in the misery that to be this far from home
Means there is no home to return to
I cling to photographs
Text messages I feel inadequate to respond
And the occasional phone call

Sell rich fantasies
of being safe and in good health
When truly I have descended beneath the soil
Into the land of perpetual solitude
With my arms outstretched to keep my balance
Stinking of ash and sweat
Stinking of apathy
Turned into a blinded beggar
A leeching parasite
Come to feed off the decaying roots
of a fallen empire.

I want to love the people whom I love
I want to keep loving the people whom I love
I want to take them out for beers on a warm day
And drink wine in the kitchen
And go to the bathhouse and have tea afterwards
I want to go for walks by the lakes or the harbor
And kiss each other hurriedly on the bus stop
I want to sit in the sun and laugh about the things we don't like
I want to give them plants they'll forget to water
and silly drawings I made
And let them borrow my clothes
And borrow their clothes and never give them back
And skinny-dip at midnight
I want to lay in bed and watch bad reality shows
Go out dancing and hold hands whilst walking home
And I want to be better at showing vulnerability
And let them all know how much I love them
And I want to make mistakes and be called out
And be held tightly when I'm anxious because it's what they saw
on *Grey's Anatomy*
And tell them that I had forgotten how to miss people until now
I want to go on road trips
and make out in small-town supermarkets
And make fun of them when they are ashy
And laugh until our stomachs hurt
And talk about films and art and politics
And open the door for each other late at night

And share an orange on a bench
And be sorry when I am rude
And tell each other the times we had our hearts broken
And go to the park and learn how to ride a bike
And have Christmas dinner in pajamas
And give presents they reluctantly accept
And tell each other how we were as children
And tell each other the times we had our hearts put back together
And eat ice cream by the canals
I want to be there when they are sad
And sit with them until they're better
And talk on the phone for hours
I wish the world was a different place for people like us
And work on creating safety for each other
And forgiving each other when we disappoint
And hold each other close despite our thorns
And wash the dishes in the morning
And be each other's muses
And take pictures when we're happy
And realize that love is not meant to bind people to each other
And feel grateful to have experienced
To still experience it
Although it is volatile and unpredictable
I am deeply fortunate to have felt
How blindingly beautiful it is.

Do not touch my hair.

Stop asking me what I think about *Lemonade*.

We lied when we said you look good with box braids

You know nothing about our struggle.

Why do you kiss your dogs? They lick their own ass.

Is clapping to a beat really that hard?

Why do you wear those ugly Jesus sandals?

Why does your food have the same complexion as your skin?

Why do you listen to Black music that

Black people don't listen to any more?

Jazz does not belong to you.

Adele is not that good.

Neither is Macklemore.

Why are you so awkward all the fucking time?

Why do you think you know more Black people than Black people?

Stop giving us goods past their expiration date and calling it charity.

Why do you say "All lives matter"?

Why is it attractive to look like a child?

Why don't you respect your elders?

Why do you shame people of color for their food

then make a trend out of it?

Why are you so hostile to immigrants?

Why do you feel the need to protect your national identity

when you are so devoid of any culture?

Why do you paint us as violent and aggressive

when you are responsible for so many deaths?

Why do you smile at people like you're walking past them
at the post office?
Why do you hold coffee mugs with two hands, close your eyes
as you drink and utter "mmmmmm"?
Why do you vote for nationalists?
Tell me how much you love your job
And missionary sex
And weird porn
And tell me
Why do you fantasize about Black dicks?
And call the police on Black people?
Clutch your purse when we walk past you?
Why do you deny that racism exists?
Why do you ask us why we're angry all the time?
Here is a better question for you: Do you ever just feel grateful that
what we want is equality and not revenge?

DON'T YOU EVER FEEL GRATEFUL THAT ALL WE WANT IS EQUALITY AND NOT REVENGE
DON'T YOU EVER FEEL GRATEFUL THAT ALL WE WANT IS EQUALITY AND NOT REVENGE
DON'T YOU EVER FEEL GRATEFUL THAT ALL WE WANT IS EQUALITY AND NOT REVENGE
DON'T YOU EVER FEEL GRATEFUL THAT ALL WE WANT IS EQUALITY AND NOT REVENGE
DON'T YOU EVER FEEL GRATEFUL THAT ALL WE WANT IS EQUALITY AND NOT REVENGE
DON'T YOU EVER FEEL GRATEFUL THAT ALL WE WANT IS EQUALITY AND NOT REVENGE
DON'T YOU EVER FEEL GRATEFUL THAT ALL WE WANT IS EQUALITY AND NOT REVENGE
DON'T YOU EVER FEEL GRATEFUL THAT ALL WE WANT IS EQUALITY AND NOT REVENGE
DON'T YOU EVER FEEL GRATEFUL THAT ALL WE WANT IS EQUALITY AND NOT REVENGE
DON'T YOU EVER FEEL GRATEFUL THAT ALL WE WANT IS EQUALITY AND NOT REVENGE
DON'T YOU EVER FEEL GRATEFUL THAT ALL WE WANT IS EQUALITY AND NOT REVENGE
DON'T YOU EVER FEEL GRATEFUL THAT ALL WE WANT IS EQUALITY AND NOT REVENGE
DON'T YOU EVER FEEL GRATEFUL THAT ALL WE WANT IS EQUALITY AND NOT REVENGE
DON'T YOU EVER FEEL GRATEFUL THAT ALL WE WANT IS EQUALITY AND NOT REVENGE
DON'T YOU EVER FEEL GRATEFUL THAT ALL WE WANT IS EQUALITY AND NOT REVENGE
DON'T YOU EVER FEEL GRATEFUL THAT ALL WE WANT IS EQUALITY AND NOT REVENGE
DON'T YOU EVER FEEL GRATEFUL THAT ALL WE WANT IS EQUALITY AND NOT REVENGE
DON'T YOU EVER FEEL GRATEFUL THAT ALL WE WANT IS EQUALITY AND NOT REVENGE
DON'T YOU EVER FEEL GRATEFUL THAT ALL WE WANT IS EQUALITY AND NOT REVENGE
DON'T YOU EVER FEEL GRATEFUL THAT ALL WE WANT IS EQUALITY AND NOT REVENGE
DON'T YOU EVER FEEL GRATEFUL THAT ALL WE WANT IS EQUALITY AND NOT REVENGE
DON'T YOU EVER FEEL GRATEFUL THAT ALL WE WANT IS EQUALITY AND NOT REVENGE
DON'T YOU EVER FEEL GRATEFUL THAT ALL WE WANT IS EQUALITY AND NOT REVENGE
DON'T YOU EVER FEEL GRATEFUL THAT ALL WE WANT IS EQUALITY AND NOT REVENGE
DON'T YOU EVER FEEL GRATEFUL THAT ALL WE WANT IS EQUALITY AND NOT REVENGE
DON'T YOU EVER FEEL GRATEFUL THAT ALL WE WANT IS EQUALITY AND NOT REVENGE
DON'T YOU EVER FEEL GRATEFUL THAT ALL WE WANT IS EQUALITY AND NOT REVENGE
DON'T YOU EVER FEEL GRATEFUL THAT ALL WE WANT IS EQUALITY AND NOT REVENGE

Souls wandering around chained to a system
that forbids us to look beyond the green notes
Like death feels good.
Chasing after paper
that polishes the sharp-toothed smiles of greed
whilst we grind on that minimum wage
broken down field niggers in blue collars
In this world

Where we are still monkeys with less humanity than the animal
In this world.
where bullet holes in brown skin spark no outrage.
In this world
Where children play alongside dead bodies holding meth pipes
In this world

The whip cracks on the school-to-prison pipeline
In the mass incarceration and perpetual genocide of the brownskins
in the destabilized regions across the world
that set the scene for a colonization that never ends.
From the missionaries that give us old T-shirts and bibles
to the tragic caricatures of the people they have condemned
with a promise of salvation
then tyrannize the meek us for the sake of righteousness
For theirs is Earth to inherit.

For ours is Earth to inherit.
In this world
where we have been punished for sins we have not committed
Brutalized and silenced
we're still here
Heartbroken and enraged
we're still here
We know what hellfire feel like
we're still here

'Cause we too resilient to bow our heads
not in this time
Not in this life
'cause our deaths are no coincidence
And our rage will not go unnoticed
Still victorious 'cause we didn't perish.
Coming out of this black pool
Throwing our heads back, laughing
and set in determination to keep going
looking death in the face and say
We made it
We made it
We made it . . .

ACKNOWLEDGMENTS

An enormous thanks to Mette Moestrup for your infallible guidance, support, friendship, and collaborations. A huge thanks to my lovely editor Julie Paludan-Müller and my incredible kick-ass agent, Szilvia Molnar. Thank you Farhiya Khalid, I am always marveled by your sharp intelligence and kindness and for putting me on to Oumou Sangare. And thank you Nadia Nadesan for helping me write this acknowledgment.

ABOUT THE AUTHOR

Aaiún Nin (born 1991) is a writer, mixed media artist, and painter born in Luanda, Angola. Aaiún's poetry has been published in multiple Scandinavian magazines and journals, including *Information*, *(un)told pages*, *Kritiker*, *Friktion*, *Forfatternes Klimaaksjon*, and hvermandag.dk. They are also the contributing editor of the Danish magazine *Marronage*. They have performed and read at literary festivals such as the Oslo Internasjonale Poesifestival in Norway and the Louisiana Literature Festival in Denmark. The leading Danish newspaper *Politiken* called Nin a "great, rare talent in Danish literature." They studied in Zimbabwe and South Africa before moving to Denmark. They currently reside in Krakow, Poland.

It takes a village to get from a manuscript to the printed book in your hands. The team at Astra House would like to thank everyone who helped to publish *Broken Halves of a Milky Sun*.

PUBLISHER
Ben Schrank

EDITORIAL
Alessandra Bastagli
Olivia Dontsov

CONTRACTS
Stefanie Ratzki

PUBLICITY
Rachael Small

MARKETING
Tiffany Gonzalez
Sarah Christensen Fu
Jordan Snowden

SALES
Jack W. Perry

DESIGN
Jacket: Rodrigo Corral Studio
Interior: Richard Oriolo
Jeanette Tran

PRODUCTION
Lisa Taylor
Alisa Trager
Rebecca Baumann

COPYEDITING
Janine Barlow

COMPOSITION
Westchester Publishing Services

ABOUT ASTRA HOUSE

Astra House is dedicated to publishing authors across genres and from around the world. We value works that are authentic, ask new questions, present counter-narratives and original thinking, challenge our assumptions, and broaden and deepen our understanding of the world. Our mission is to advocate for authors who experience their subject deeply and personally, and who have a strong point of view; writers who represent multifaceted expressions of intellectual thought and personal experience, and who can introduce readers to new perspectives about their everyday lives as well as the lives of others.